Before Them, We

an anthology

edited by Ruth Sutoyé
and Jacob Sam-La Rose

flipped eye publishing
London

Before Them, We

First published in 2022 by flipped eye publishing | www.flippedeye.net

Compilation © 2022 Ruth Sutoyé and Jacob Sam-La Rose
Cover Design © flipped eye publishing, 2022
Cover Photo © Adama Jalloh
Author Photo © Gifty Dzenyo
Photo credits © Ruth Sutoyé

This book is typeset in Book Antiqua and Palatino Linotype

Printed and bound in Great Britain.

ISBN- 978-1-905233-77-9

Supported using public funding by
ARTS COUNCIL
ENGLAND
LOTTERY FUNDED

Before Them, We

an anthology

edited by Ruth Sutoyé
and Jacob Sam-La Rose

Table of Contents

FOREWORD

Before Them, We is an offering for memory and for the preservation of African diaspora familial histories. An offering to my late grandmother, who serves as the inspiration. This anthology exists as part of a larger multidisciplinary project, including a photography exhibition and poetry film. Together, the anthology and the wider project serve as a poetic and visual meditation on how we engage with the practice of memory, and a tribute to the archive; as an ode to the life stories of elders who were/are lesser known; an ode to grief and to an ongoing regret derived from not being able to document the many life stories my grandmother had shared with me before her passing.

The notion of community is fundamental to the social and cultural power of storytelling and to represent any sense of the community and communities through this body of work, it was vital to showcase varied and shared experiences. This anthology constitutes a community of UK based poets and storytellers of African descent, a community of writers and thinkers ranging from Gen Z to preceding generations, writers and thinkers who could contribute to and be meaningfully impacted by this offering. They have mined and made peace with, interrogated, unpicked, circled around and sought for a myriad ways to approach their family histories, the personal stories and mythologies of figures who came before them. However close or far removed from their subjects, these writers have walked into those stories and myths, finding ways to come to terms with the flesh and blood (and in some cases the absences) behind them.

Poetry is a perfect vehicle for this effort; allowing for the lines that separate fact and fiction to be traversed and even transgressed in search of deeper truths. The way a poem's lens can focus on a singular view of a seminal moment or scene, or extend to embrace conflicting layers of the same constructed self becomes part of the reader's journey. The photographic work within this anthology consists of images I made of some of the families featured in the exhibition. There is something undeniably mortal about being able to witness three or more generations of family members in still or moving images, perhaps even something to be envied or coveted. This is a perspective not everyone is able to experience and I hope this work functions in part as a call to action for readers to fiercely protect the histories of their families, to pass much more of them on to future generations - much like African traditions have carried stories forward orally for centuries. Being able to facilitate this collective form of archiving with these poetic voices has been one of my greatest joys.

Contributing to the Black, African, Diasporic canon and honouring our elders in a way that captures their narratives permanently was one of my larger objectives. I hope that readers find stories they relate to or recognise, stories that speak to their own pre-histories, stories that inspire them to dig deeper, ask more, do more to enshrine the lived experiences of their grandparents and forebears whilst those elders are still alive, or be fervent in the pursuit of creating a lasting manifestation of their legacies if those elders have since passed.

Ruth Sutoyé

EBI

Photography by Ruth Sutoyé, selected from a wider series of images exhibited at the Black Cultural Archives in 2021, as part of the Before Them, We visual installation. Portraiture exploring intergenerational relationships between family members of African descent based in the UK.

Image I: legacy

TOLU AGBELUSI

Amongst its many uses, poetry for me is a place to be still enough to observe and find meaning in pockets of life that might otherwise be overlooked. It is an opportunity to excavate, record and retell histories. In my adulthood, I am reckoning with the fact that there is much I do not know about my parents' early lives, many assumptions borne out of the tensions of parent/child relationships, and so many fragments of stories I didn't sufficiently value at the point of its telling, to retain. Before it is too late to return to the people they were and sit inside the joy of reminiscence, I have begun to interview them about their lives. These poems draw inspiration from that process of rediscovery in the context of understanding familial connections between generations and their influence on our lives now, even in the diaspora.

Tell Me All the Stories. This Time I'll Remember

When I meet my grandfather for the first time,
he has been dead for almost a hundred years.

Middle-aged, in visibly well-worn shoes, he counts
all the dirty, torn notes in his wallet. Pockets too.

Hands over the school fees at St Finbarr's College,
Lagos. In full. Then petitions: *Sir, can I see Dele. Tell him*

it's his driver. He is aware that those affirmed by privilege
would find insult at his audacity in claiming this world

for his son. When the boy who is not yet my father arrives
Grandad silences his confusion with a whisper—

                                        nobody needs to know

The boy has always known. When his father lowers
himself onto the courtyard stool, sews yet another patch

on his threadbare agbada, the only one he owns, assures
his son tomorrow will live up to its promise, they know.

What manner of man puffs his chest at the expense
of his children? Not Grandad. *Poverty is a thing of the mind.*

He refused to be the reason his son became a laughingstock.
He chose surrender—of status, pride, the right to respond

to the tongues lashing him out of the space reserved
for those deemed worthy. When I meet my grandfather

Tolu Agbelusi

for the first time, in this story, I am interviewing my father
at the dinner table. He recalls the way silence occupied him

for the rest of the school day. The long walk home,
the moment his body found a bed. The way he wept, finally

coming into the knowledge of how much his father had to let go,
just to make sure his children had a childhood without lack,

one he never knew. So many years later, the memory
conjures him, steals my father's voice.

Origin Stories

What's in a name? My grandaddy watched his father reduce his mother to a bloody heap. Some memories refuse to wither, grow with a boy until he is a man. Grandad stripped himself of his father's name. One of many things he would shed. By the time I chose to wear Bababode, the sting, like the old man, was long gone.

*

We move. Great Grandma left the village with nothing but her children and the certainty there was more to life than waiting for the angry fist that would end her.

*

There was that one uncle who delighted in telling your mother, if you marry him, it will fall apart. *The night before she said* I do, *playing his curse on repeat, she decided—whatever aches the future may unveil, returning home would never be one.*

*

It has never been about a place.

*

Ask my daughter. She will tell you I go where the Spirit leads. A voice. A leaning. Once, I mooted possibilities of drastic change—no drivers, no big houses, little comfort. She advised I check again with God, why it was that we should have to suffer.

*

We didn't run from Nigeria. When I told your mother what I heard in prayer, her face was a call to attention. In the land where doors only open with an exchange of names. Of notes. Not a friend was called for assistance. No currency exchanged. We refused to help God. Call it a dare. Or faith. The visa refused for two years running arrived in two weeks. We were not desperate. I am not sorry to disappoint you.

Tolu Agbelusi

Gabriel Akamo

NB *Please read the poems first, then come back*

As someone with no surviving grandparents, somewhat disconnected from the extended family before my parents' generation, I found writing these poems particularly challenging. While I deeply wanted to document or, in some sense, preserve the lives, stories, and histories of family before they were family, I didn't feel I could before working on these. Part of the process involved a group session exploring different forms of narratology — the study of narrative, including the various types of non-, anti-, post-narrative. That session with the editors and other writers in this anthology gave me the confidence to choose to write that ambiguity and second-handedness into the poems — particularly Pontiac. The recollection of a life is just that: re- collecting; and the pieces, gaps, and arrangement of those determine the telling of the story and, in turn, the story itself. Therefore, my intent was to document from a place of not knowing, learning, and then collecting/assembling again.

Pontiac (read it first) is about my great-grandfather's murder, following his involvement in politics. By the time of his death his daughter (my maternal grandmother) was already a parent. For this reason, I wasn't sure whether this counted as a before them (being children and grandchildren), but it felt important to write this anyway. All I know about his life is how he lost it, so from my generation's perspective, there is no before. But I don't think that matters.

íwín is for my maternal grandfather. As a child he returned home one day to find his mother and siblings dead (suspected poisoning). This led to a childhood of hard labour and abuse from his caregivers, resulting in his struggling to stay awake in school (and deafness in one ear). Despite this, he excelled academically, acing a medical school entrance exam [a year] before he was eligible for it, and won a scholarship to study in Britain where he became a doctor. (How he was entered for the exam is unclear). He also maintained a cheerful demeanour, a habit of whistling and — as I learned shortly before writing this — an obsession with the works of Shakespeare.

íwín

returning home to find the whole house dark,
the moon and stars cold, in a crumpled heap.

his mother would still speak to him in dreams
and when he'd fall asleep in class then wake to catch the teacher out.
once, he stopped the cane mid-flight with just a word.

no wonder his boys would cheer and call him *íwín*:
the sprite. tiny man of miracles, who'd
make a life of making people whole,

suck bad vibes from a room and never break a sweat.
he even dreamt the antidote to death
and bottled all the bad luck in the world.

Gabriel Akamo

She used herself as a ~~body~~ shield
until the ~~assassins~~

   ~~men~~

   political thugs

        opening fire, splintered the door, paused
shoved her out of the way   and bulleted him
there, killing him   in cold blood.

         (By the time ~~they~~ the family, th
         arrived, the ~~Party~~

          political thugs had le
        ~~Judas~~ ~~Simon Peter~~
        ~~begging his body~~ weeping ove

        ~~It is said~~ the burnt Pontiac
        remains, a ~~shadow~~
         monument ~~forever~~
          to this da

  i.

Before?
There ~~had never been~~
   can never be   a grander father. *The* Otunba:
Heir-Elect. A political giant so great, Death's desperate
darts missed him (at least) thrice before. He knew
the plot, and locked down the house. His guards and family: ready.
his friend phoned desperate and distressed. *I'm coming.*
His guards begged to go with him, but nobly, he refused. Then vanished
from their sight.

When he appeared with the Pontiac,
the friend's wife rushed out of the house,
embraced him and clinging tight, he left the key in the ignition
and entered a side room of the house.

crying *t'ẹ bá y'ibon, èmi l'ẹ kọkọ́ ma pá*

even the car, that's why / they left the car

guards,   everyone

ft.

he "friend" stayed

him.   *aaaah! Pọjú!*

y)

(King)

Then

mo ń bọ̀.

irọ́ ni o! irọ́ ni! wọn fẹ pa! wọn fẹ pa!

the car

Gabriel Akamo

Asmaa Jama

The writing was inspired by me trying to reconcile the histories in my family, histories involving migration + water. In *autopsy*, I was trying to re-imagine my grandfather's funeral, one we never attended. The distance in my family caused my displacement, makes mourning a strange experience. How do you mourn someone you've never met, how do you remember?

In *learning to swim*, the poem is inspired by a verse I heard sung by Maryan Mursal / my father would sing it a lot growing up. Recently I've been thinking a lot about myths, surrounding waters / coastline in Somalia. I thought of all the ways we are pulled to the sea.

autopsy

at the end, my grandfather is somehow still together, bones and loose flesh, splayed viscera in a plane seat, he arrives at our home like a decorated war vet, except he has only survived himself, except no nation now wants him, except he has only battled against the tide and has lost every time, except he is missing all of his hair and most of his teeth

and when i see him i collapse into my own shadow, and our house becomes filled with bodies again for the funeral

except this time, i reconstruct his image, i hand over my packaged skin, my viscera and my grandfather takes an almost alive shape

and we attend the funeral together, already there is oil being spilt into the ground, which is just the zaytun's way of mourning him, and after eating pickled chillies, we drink until our insides cool

at dawn this time i perform, his autopsy, i place my hand into the palace of his skin, and find, in its lines, the intestines, that have swollen into small galaxies, pregnant lengths

and i write them odes, i write them fragile odes, somehow spilling ink onto his body, somehow pressing words, like chosen, and once-loved

and the word for forgiveness and the word for blessing remain the same, and there is a slow rain that falls over his body, which is really the earth washing him, as i tuck him away, like he is spilt taffeta, and my hands are rippling

and then i go to dig at the earth until it at last opens, and then i wrap him in cloth, and then we press our foreheads to his ground, which is everywhere, and later the clouds part

and of course this is a false body, and of course it dissipates as i fold him, leaving only wet cotton, leaving only myself performing empty ceremonies, hollow gestures, hollow language burnt up and out

Asmaa Jama

and all my syllables are half torn by grief, and my prayers return to me, asking to be sewn together to be made more coherent things, except i have no utterances for god only gestures, i raise my palm to my chest, i place a finger to my head, and my ocular bone, and all the places that ripple and turn water

i want for better things, for peace, i want for smaller things, for a semblance of a grave stone, for one more missed call and the sound of his voice, for misbegotten camel hide

i ask again for his solid body, for malachite strong fingers, for a will to continue, and even my grandfather tired of my trope, tired of returning in a wearisome body sends smaller creatures, green amphibians, dark silent millipedes at last a single goldfish

which is his way of asking for rest, which is his way for asking for peace, for an end to my constant surveillance, and the uttering of his name, in my mouth, which is his way of saying you are a stranger, hardly a grandchild

after you crossed the water, i lost your face, pale photograph in a well

learning to swim

what are you but the body of water that has tried to own me three times
maryan sings, her face dripping

outside my aunt's apartment building cutting up the night, lit matches everywhere, flaming windows
and lit matches everywhere, tongue gasoline

which is the only thing that floats in the sea, that can stand to, i reach out and touch a face almost like mine, and we dig at the earth, until it is warm and wet, until it is ready to be made brittle, bone-dry with flame

maryan sang, my shadow, in all this water, who owns my name,
my father pulled us away from the coastline, until our limbs bloated

and we were afraid, so we used the tide like it was a tether, and we came back sand-filled
i'm sure the sea is exhausted of me mentioning its name, and never writing any elegies–
sea, who folds in its mouth the teeming everyone made to cross water

and wasn't it my grandfather who sat in his house, its corrugated tin roofs, away from water, sat inside, when it rained, let the camels' fur grow damp, let them come in roves looking for shelter

and in nairobi, didn't my grandmother hold our mouths open to water, as if it was the sea being cut out of the air, and didn't we bleach our sheets white, clean after the cats, fill our scars, call it salt and a blessing

the sea, already thirty-five parts salt, could not consume us even if it wanted to, my father whispered, and held our fingers and told us float

and they all knew how to swim, or they said that they did, said they were always at the mouth, at the coastline, and they went in arms raised

Asmaa Jama

and my uncle was the only one who knew how to collect fish, strew their mouths open, and make them small fruitful dawns

i mean my uncle was a boat, freshly carved, beautiful in water

i mean my uncle was forever dappled and damp, on land, he sat with his palms, to his ocular bone, held it closed, and it kept leaking, and i could never tell if it was because of me, or the tear gas

my uncle a moored boat, landlocked, lies in a shallow bath, of water, he keeps telling us, he can chart the globe, he keeps telling us that the night is clear

he can flatten the sea, like a bedsheet and we ask him to stay

whole in nairobi, say we have no more flames, can do no more ceremonies for the gone, and he does, wood turning soft, soft body in decay

SIANA BANGURA

Like many writers from an immigrant background, I am preoccupied with matters of identity; belonging, family histories; the intersections of race, class, and gender; and of course religion – or lack thereof.

Across both of these poems, as with much of my writing in this season, there is a strong theme of water. As well as water being deeply meaningful in West African cultures (among others), it is a sign of rebirth and renewal, of life as well as death. It is often associated with birth, fertility, and refreshment. In a Christian context, water has many correlations, for example: Christ walking on water; transforming this element into wine, and of course baptism. Human beings are roughly seventy percent water (as is the earth's surface, coincidentally) and so water is closely associated with transcendence of the earthly condition. In many ways, the characters in these poems are trying to, or have already, transcended their own earthly condition.

Sprinklers

The church swelters as the pastor speaks of hellfire in dulcet tones
swears utter damnation on any beast who turns their back on a living Lord
stained glass windows foggy with condensation
and the tears of women and girls who become slaves to holy men

Bags of change rustle with familiarity
demands for weekly tithe fill the dense air
aunties fan their heavily made up faces
regal lace wet with salty sweat
head wraps like ice cream melting in cones

To our surprise the heavens open
sprinklers and alarms erupt like a burst dam
kneeling cushions transfigure into life jackets
our aunties float like balloons on water

Torrents roar between the church walls
like hundreds of rivers searching for the sea

Our aunties become weaving water snakes
criss-crossing between oak valleys
Mami Wata's own reflection
makeup, hair and fabrics dripping into puddles, streams, oceans

Despite the pandemonium, nobody dares to scream
between swipes to clear our eyes from storms
our palms rise to the skies
children hide under pews
the jollof and chicken float in their aluminium boats
red cups now cleats without a rope

As quickly as the sky opened its gut
the showers come to an end
the pastor lays prostrate
with joy we draw water out of the wells of salvation
the congregation falls to their knees

We rejoice as if it were a baptism

Grandma – Part II

i

Years have passed since that first poem.
I told my readers you were a terrible mother.
Against the grain of West African sensibility,
I aired the family's dirty laundry.

As for the other mothers?
The bitter and twisted have been buried.
Their flesh returned to the earth.
Nobody attended their funerals except the pastor and pallbearers.
A prayer was said as their souls transitioned
into expectant air.

Our apologetic mothers, too, have now gone,
their hearts finally burst like a dam from the weight of the river.
Their children attended the funerals dutifully.
Temperate tears morphed into tropical rainforests,
lumps in throat,
seasonal swell.

ii

In these moments, the family story was written.
Your own mother denied your dreams,
did not let you dance in the wind to sweet music,
oscillate in the Atlantic breeze.

Your husband denied your daughters greener pastures.
Against my dead body he declared.

The cruelty of the irony is never lost on me -
war in the blood for generations to come.
What is home without a mother?
Your children turned mud and water into stones.
The heart blisters to think of it -
the incalculable untended to wounds,
each root of the family tree an archive.

iii

We are left searching for answers,
scrambling over shards nobody will take with them.
When you meet your maker,
He will ask about your regrets.

You have waited epochs to finally exhale -
You will share the intricate alphabet of your heart,
tell Him you wish you had found a way
to rewrite the chapters of your family's book.

You died too many times before this one.
Before you had the chance to make your wrongs right.
Before one final trip to the ocean…
Before joy could return…
before…
before…
before…

Siana Bangura

Dzifa Benson

As I get older, it has become more and more important to explore my family history in my writing because I am separated from the intricacies of my cultural heritage by living in Europe. This is the way I compensate for not being fluent in Ewe, the Ghanaian language that my family speaks. My ear understands Ewe very well but when I try to speak it, the feeling is akin to a kind of paralysis in the pathways between my brain and my tongue. The irony is that I'm attempting to counteract that loss of the Ewe language with a language, English, in which I feel supremely articulate. So writing about near and distant ancestors (the Anthonys and the Attipoes), particularly the female ones, and refracting their origin stories, mythologies and modes of discourse through my imagination feels very grounding because it means I'm holding tight to an Ewe identity even within the paucity of my knowledge of the language. I chose the song-like form of the ghazal form to facilitate this and it is inherent in a title like *Myself, When I'm Real*.

Echolalia: A Broken Rule Ghazal

For the Anthonys and for the Attipoes

This is the place. I am here. These are their names, unsaid in water.
This tree stump, kidi the mother drum, blazons blood shed in water.

Walking barefoot and backwards through the grinding sands of Ketume
rainwater bites and saltwater laughs at Keta straight ahead, in water.

In Amedzofe, the nucleus of the calabash that holds a mirror
to the sky is Dukli's stern face in a black top hat misread in water.

I must press my query into the honeycomb of coral, this talisman
gifted from Florencia, to craft a rope of clay, unread in water.

When the waves curdle at my feet, Patience, the tailor's fifth wife
hands me Sokpewo, the warm stones of god, to tread in water.

Elnathan the court clerk in broad brimmed hat and lace up ankle boots
scattered his seeds to the ends of the earth and widespread in water.

Matilda's ghost still sits on her wooden stool by the hurricane lamp
her Star Beer and Dutch wax print dye, runs froth-red in water.

The sly smiles of yet another Philemon curse the cresting lungs
of the ravenous Atlantic as it washes away his homestead in water.

My tongue cooks like that time Vicenzia scrubbed laterite soil on
to my gums the way Adekpui carved the wet wall's breach bred in water.

Let it grow for longer sang Cecilia to tighten-your-waist drumming
when they crossed the T-junction to Agorko, coils shed in water.

Dzifa Benson

The Berlin Conference decreed Brandina another country.
She's the charcoal of a burnt coconut plantation, dread in water.

Sit on the stool? Dzifa's body only believes what it can feel,
the corn dough of mother tongue, a song of self, not dead in water.

Myself, When I Am Real

'Woman accidentally joins a search party looking for herself'

When I was Xetsa, the African Grey, I said:
even if I am bleeding, please look
at my red tail feathers. You'll find I'm still whole.

I was my twin Evi, void and bellyful at the same time.
Raging and hungry as the grey sea,
my throat closed like dough that can't rise.

I was cousin Kafui when every moon was blue.
What was the word going round and round
in my head? I let it dry on me like a wet shirt.

I was loving Vincenzia, despair sitting fat inside, rearing
its jaundiced head. I wasn't lost but I set myself free.
Living loud in my elsewhere, I became the last girl, Mansa.

My mother's voice said 'Remember Noona, a little bit
of fuchsia lipstick changes your day.' I spent my time wishing
I was a wolf with its soft underbelly and its big animal gaze.

Now I am Brandina, my great-great grandmother. I spread
myself so thin and green, I am an elephant's back in Phuket,
a beach in Anloga, a discarded shoe in Boston.

Through the wing of a dragonfly, I point to darkness.
Soon I will become Fafali, the youngest.

Dzifa Benson

CLEMENTINE BURNLEY

In Britain people consider the current moment of pandemic uncertainty, of movement across borders or frustration with political leaderships, or uncertainty in the economic markets a new thing but this is what many people outside Europe have been living for a long time. These poems are a meditation on how things are going, in places outside the mainstream.

I wanted to take a look at the details of individual lives against a wide canvas. Both poems reflect relationships lived out on the move, momentary connections and partings. Both are set in the 1990s. At the time, the homes where I grew up felt like a train station. Someone was always arriving and someone was always leaving. I slept on the sofa a lot. The adults stayed up until the small hours talking about family and about world events which at the time seemed remote. The world seems smaller now.

Broken English

The Bow bells sound faint
against the broken air conditioning unit.
Cushions have abandoned this sofa
as sleep has abandoned the dark.
She carries a letter in my grandmother's
copperplate script.
Big voice for a small woman,
this early rising, suitcase trading,
Blood-of-Jesus-old woman
who has taken my bed.
How powerful must we be,
to break an empire's language
without firing a single shot.
Her eyes are the dark reflective blue
of magpies, cataracts
or the grey stars of approaching blindness.
When she speaks, I do not understand.
She must have her reasons
for unleashing all the miscellaneous,
motley words I will never speak.
What we're not talking about
is what I need to survive.
I do not know how to say 'English'
in all the tongues I do not speak.

Clementine Burnley

The Book of Revelations

(for Francois K. and Alice U.)

The shadow jet skims terraced fields of sorghum
millet and sweet potato. Armageddon is a place

in the New Testament, until rockets climb the evening,
and clouds stand back for April.

Suppose instead of missiles, eagles mount
the darkening sky.

A jet completes its final approach
instead of a fireball descent.

A cadet returns to his station.
Suppose a nation breathes.

Instead, an engine note descends into the red.
Armageddon is a day in April: two presidents die.

Tomorrow, children will ford bloodied rivers.
Everyone in the foreign press is watching Mandela

because finally something good is happening in Africa.
The flattened dial tone when you try to ring
means home, unobtainable.

This day in April, a bugle calls cadets to order.
This day is for the bludgeon and the blade.

In the future, pilgrims will congregate on the grounds of a memorial.
Generations to come will see their kin through different eyes.

In the future, when you lift a boy into a playground swing
you close your eyes as he ascends into an innocent sky.

Clementine Burnley

Ola Elhassan

These poems are about my Grandmother, Amal Galal El-Ibs, someone whose stories I keep revisiting for answers like in *Glissade*. I didn't know much about her life before us. Luckily, I found old emails with word documents from my grandfather. He'd sent them when she passed, with details about their life together and captioned photos of her "in the newly installed Power Samas, a punch card based system installed by Sudan Railways in Atbara over 50 years ago. It was used for stock taking, salaries and other punch card accounting"

In *Atbara as Coefficients* I took the facts I learned about her and life in Atbara. Using the shape of a coefficient matrix to hold scattered information, they preface a vector matrix where the variables are her name in some of the many cities she lived in. When the two multiply, they mimic how the memory or the same story can reoccur in different instances of our lives to mean new things - in a less stagnant way than a list or paragraph. The diagonal is italicised as a play on identity matrices and eigen-values as the root of a system.

Atbara as Coefficients

the hydrology of the Atbara
river says it is usually a stream
starting from South-East

of arid ground and Sudan's
polyrhythms walking the
markets

mandarin lemonad
pink one and the or
on tap from your c
house

with Egyptian marching
bands and monomythic
English jazz on the radio

*known as the city of iron and
fire with domed houses for its
workers*

where your mother
from a village furth
called Number Six

where the Ibs family
distributed lemonade for
Sudan Railway

where tea was made in the
yard with a gas powered
babour

*fragrant garden you s
dream under a bare m*

where the breakfast whistle
called you home for warm
beans with cumin and
sesame oil

where you marbled two
cakes with orange zest into
three tins

the first place you l
good

and the   where the afternoon whistle
nge one   called the town home for
usin's   rest

settled   the home that we never saw
r north   in Alsawdana with trees to
    walk with

ept in to   where you and your sisters
ght sky   crossed river stems on
    bicycles to play tennis

ft for   *where you were born*

امال Atbara

امال Khartoum

امال London

امال Edinburgh

Ola Elhassan

INUA ELLAMS

I have an evolving relationship with poetry. At times, I have tried to eviscerate a reader or an audience with it, tried to entertain, beguile, befuddle, illuminate, pacify, even - in my most juvenile of days - preach. With growth comes awareness, of my ability to understand, of my limitations, and in that, humility. All I try to do with poetry now, is to bear witness, to the ways the world has been, the ways it is, and ways it might yet become; to notate the melodies and narratives that have sung us into our present being. With these poems, I tried to explore what was before we became, and what becoming unleashed within our humanity. Both feature witnesses that cut across space and time, both touch down in Nigeria, the land of my birth.

Of / Firmaments and Fractals

Before all else / in the ages of darkness / the firmaments and fractals who after its construction / gifted selfhood to man / did not consider that pharaohs would think of slaves hefting rocks up half-built pyramids / what a Muslim scholar would write of naked Vikings in tenth century Scandinavia / cavorting after squealing pigs / his nose turned up / like colonial Christian soldiers at bare-chested West Africans pouring from thatched huts / spears at the ready / drums beating a primal pattern / Gen Z rappers in pristine sneakers would claim to hear / while mocking dust-streaked untouchable kids south-east of Nepal banging on tin-pan drums / All this cosmic witnesses track / to beam / back as evidence / urging fractals and firmaments / to consider gifts other than selfhood / before all else

All the / Songs

1896 / My ancestor is a ten-year-old child of elegance vexed by the rain spattering her feet / She turns for solutions from her father / finds the suitor she hopes to love ogling /

She coughs out the welling joy in her mouth and leaves the field / Inland / dawn sweeps across the kingdom / across the pristine streets / smoothed edges of stone / the slabs warming on the path she takes /

She darts past open rooms / where younger girls of the palace practice breathing from the belly / the steps to hold and push out a sombre note / The novice wailers hang on each dirge's turn and my ancestor trembles with their song /

Weeks before / when her mother explained strange tracks smoother and thinner than feet / were found surrounding the kingdom and she and a pool of wise women / knew what danger had come / she promised to forget the songs / warn her father /

Months after / when the maxim guns glint and the British open fire / my ancestor who is captured downhill / to be bound among the loot and cattle / hears the wailers sing through a siege of canon-shell and burning and roars / as their spirits soar in smoke /

In the flickering bronze of a room centuries later / I watch my newborn niece hushed by candle light / Her eyes wide open as if reliving battle / she frowns at the flickering fire and flame / she seethes with a passion only lava knows

IBRAHIM HIRSI

Metronome and *On Canyons and Canons* are explorations of the lives of two ancestors of mine, a grandfather and great grandmother. Although both had passed before I was born they had a great effect on their respective families and the regions they came from. These two figures were mammoth in my home and by exploring their lives, histories, journeys and poetry I hoped to understand the philosophies and experiences of pastoral Somalis who had been going through momentous social change during the last 150 years or so.

These poems are for Xirsi Aadan Ducaale who passed away in the early 1950s and Xaliimo Guuleed Maxamed who passed away in the late 1980s and Xaadsan Cali Xaydar who passed away in 2020.

Ilaahi Haw Wada Naxariisto

Metronome

The pack animal sways side to side   walks in metronome   you are there   nuzzled in the
empty air of Mudug   anti-colonialism vegetating in your lungs   so far from the struggles
that formed you   the days of the rifle   the sword   the white turbaned dervishes
the wars against the British   you think of how many people must be buried where you walk
how many gravestones were carried to sea   how many markers lay in disarray   the dead
don't care   if they are forgotten   placation is the best medicine   in all its platitudes   your
true love died on his way to Mogadishu   that was the second time nationhood was bombed
out of you   you tried to follow him   repeat a shattered journey   retrace his steps   as if he
were camel taken at night   and the expanse would carry his sound to you   let you find him
easier   but   you tasted that before   the uselessness of tracing the dead   how running
after echoes   lead you nowhere   so instead   you did the second best thing   moved back
to the life before the wars   the displacements   the Italians   the British   where unity was
not to die for   where the wind carried sulphur in its teeth   where your dreams didn't try to
humiliate you   back to when   everything didn't sound like an elegy   before you started to
confuse   your liver with your heart   still   even not every return is with fanfare   for here
having bled   for The Nation State   was considerably less fashionable   and the poetry
you memorised   was just entertainment   nothing more   so you carried whatever you
could   in that red wood box   the rest under your eyes   made sure it was known   it was
felt   that you would do as you wish   it didn't matter if your loves would taste exile   life is not
for carcasses   you reasoned   for the living to sleep in   graveyards

    Life is not for the hierarchy of coincidence   the conflict of circumstance
You hated stagnation   felt bored by   your surroundings   life was for change
you said

        And if that didn't work   a return to the beginning

On Canyons and Canons

Asceticism is gone
and I find myself
reforming the old,
treading my worn footprints.
The weed takes me
to photo albums,
those scarred pictures.
I trace gaps, ridges of emptiness.
The generation before the one
before me
was swallowed whole
by wells and war.
Displaced, they travelled
from rocky shore
to ruby plains.

Revenge sears your stomach.
I've seen it gut a nation.
Jab at spleen and gallbladder,
run through an ummah
like kidney stones.
When the
revenged upon
is not the
transgressor
but a brother of his,
it runs tracks down
generations,
leaves family trees
crooked
and lineage

Ibrahim Hirsi

cascading,
meandering.
A biological
Grand Canyon.

That's what left
him
spitting shattered
ribcage.
And the
transgressor
with lungfuls of blood
and redress.
That's what made families
pick up the rifle.
Made them
leave the sky
crackling
with yellow and
rage.

That's what broke
a generation,
left them alone,
bereft twice.
That's what turned cousins
on each other,
imbued the air
with eulogies and
white scarves of lament.
That's what melted
the gold in their teeth,
left children
lacking lip and ligament.

There are no prisons on the plains.
They wouldn't have stopped so many melting
into the clay of their origin.
In the end,
there on Ruby Plains,
justice is always followed by grief.

Ibrahim Hirsi

JANET KOFI-TSEKPO

I know little about my ancestors on my father's side. The layers of family trauma, displacement and estrangement have kept their stories hidden. I struggled to write anything that would do them any justice.

Two guides appeared. I remembered visiting Ghana many years ago. An elderly man from the Volta Region told me that my family came from a fishing village near Keta, a few miles east of where we stood. More recently, a friend I consider family suggested I research the history of saltfish. In doing so, I discovered its role within the transatlantic slave trade, and the umbilical link to Ghana within Jamaica's national dish.

Eventually, two storytellers arrived and narrated the poems. I imagine one sitting on the beach in Montego Bay and the other sailing the Keta Lagoon, connected by the Atlantic.

The History of Saltfish

Take the *akye fufo* tree, and from it the rude and ripening fruit. Feed a
man or kill a man – watch his skin crack a smile. Open him up, and you
will see the same dark seed.

Carry a man and his seed on a boat. Carry a man and his seed and the salt
cod thrown from the upper deck. Carry the man and the seed and salt cod
across the Atlantic, and it will grow and multiply.

Call it *bacalhau, bacalaítos, baccalà*. Call it solfish, like a calypsonian.
Take the memory and warm it by the fruit of the ackee tree.

Janet Kofi-Tsekpo

Me Susu Wo Lo

Long summers turn into long summers
before the rain. We fish in the lagoon
at Keta, not far from the old fort. There
the plantation was swept into the sea,
and here we pass the lighthouse at Woe.
At times we wonder how you slipped away
like stones at the sea's edge. Did you trip
and fall into the underwater mountain –
we could not say. It has been too long.
Maybe Mami Wata will return you
in a bitter swill with snakes and pearls.
Maybe a quiet wave knuckling the sand
will erode our memories of you,
like words from a language never spoken.

Esther Kondo

In astrology, Jupiter teaches us where and how we create abundance. It is associated with good fortune, healing, and has a guarding angel quality. I remember visiting a grandmother once. I say a grandmother because she was not my grandmother but she was a grandmother and I called her grandmother. She lived in the Kamba region in Kenya and did not speak much to me but showed me things. How to dig holes using my heel to plant maize; how to wash my feet before going to bed. When I heard her speak, it was under a sky showered in stars. We had gathered around a fire. Her hands— hands that have grown food, birthed, cut, gutted and milked— pointed to the fire, then the sky. I could not understand her words but I recall the words her hands made. In her eyes, I learnt how to hold fire and not burn but instead carry. Listening to these sounds and gestures taught me how to find abundance in listening.

I was raised by people that were not direct family to me. Many of the lessons that have shaped me and are shaping me came from listening and guarding resonances that reside in texts, particularly those of Audre Lorde. My poem is a practice in listening to a recording of Lorde reading at the Coolidge Auditorium in February 1982. The poem contains all the words and lines that I noted while listening to the reading in 2020. I mapped these words into a constellation to hold them in a way I could share with others. This practice of listening allows for a mapping of family that goes beyond the tree and instead resides in a galaxy of relations. Charting the stars for relatability, I draw a bond in Jupiter as I and Audre Lorde both have Libra in Jupiter in the first house.

Grains

Jewli will go home
when the maize
is ready to harvest

to burn burn
he will burn it all on hot coal
each corn a grandmother

searching the soil to scratch
a hole with the heel of her foot
feed the soil two kernels of corn

their heels a golden shovel
always in conversation with all
the backbones of all who is us

to bring nights when their children
& their children will sit around
fires adorned with

charred gold pinched in salt
teeth digging into the stars
of good fortune

9 February 1982

I - Death and renewal by fire

how shall I return   fat and beautiful
do not let me pass away   before I have a name for this tree

died too many deaths that are not mine
my children play with skulls   bones of tomorrows   fury

blackened again but this time with a sense of purpose.

II - Burned hands

pouring a pan of burning salt   a borrowed fire in her eyes   in the hungers of silence
an arrogant woman masquerading as a fish   caress the deepest bone of me   all
ghosts of me   louder than light   dark secrets from between her thighs   enchanted
fingers   dragonfish   touch the distraction within me   In the hungers of silence
the woman is eating her magic alone   begins to weep
soundlessly
     pausing to be loved

III – Midnight waters

that summer   be at home   whistling
now everything is gone   I wade through summer ghosts

grieving mothers   that summer
Clifford Glover   ancient and familiar sorrow   whistling

that summer   yam shoots   spread under high sun
trying to heal my dying sun   I wade through summer ghosts

Esther Kondo

spirits   live on in water   whistling
at home   if earth water and air do not judge them   tortured

lungs adapting to breath
 soundlessly

                                  pausing to be loved

IV - To go into madness gracefully or alone

the difference between poetry and rhetoric

Audre Lorde reading her poems
in the Coolidge Auditorium, Feb. 9, 1982

SARAH LASOYE

These two poems are written for my maternal grandmother and my mother. I didn't meet my maternal grandmother in this life. She was a remarkable person who committed herself to care for her family and community. These are commitments I share, and I'm told I resemble her in spirit and likeness which is an honour beyond the words I have. Last year, I was able to watch my parents' wedding video for the first time. It was an intensely emotional experience. In the video, my mother is 3 years older than me. I have friends who are older than she is on the screen. You can barely hear her reciting her own vows. Now though, she is loud. My wish is for her to only become louder. This project stirred so much in me. It was incredibly difficult to sit with, and to consider all the entryways into these relationships. It overwhelmed me, though eventually I remembered that these two people are whole worlds. I'm not sure why I ever thought a single poem could capture them whole. These poems are one single sketch of the space they take up in one single life (mine).

What I Have to Hold You by Is Not a Distance

for Arinlade Adelasoye

because the future turns on the balls of its feet
and I sprint by way of that
miraculous revolution
towards the staying tremor of you

it's like she was walking out of the marketplace
just as I was walking in I tell dad *it's like*
we had a conversation before I got here
but there was a hole at the bottom and I lost everything

it knots me now so when I stand
leaning against the dining table chair
distracted briefly from the ongoing problem of myself
my frame returns to a form he recognises

he arrows his relief across the room
and pins me to the wall by my shirt collar
waits for you to surface like this
like a halving cleaner than clean before he begins

if we had 1 naira no we didn't because
1 naira was 50 kobo for us and 50 for someone else
and I know this already just look at him
he carries such life with such intent

it is a joy to meet you through a movement
you named GRATITUDE TO THE STAGE
because all performance is collaboration across time
I am glad to take up this witnessing

Ye Ye

For Mum

In the wedding video your
voice is the only thing I don't
recognise in that I can barely
hear it and if your face didn't
look like that (the same) I
would   second-   guess   a
few things because yes I know
there was a time you wouldn't
speak to be heard but I prefer
the way you tell it start the
story where it gets good a shout
a call a beckoning through a
bus window the 199 the skinny
moustached man who will
become my father in the street
both of you startled by this
voice at that volume you arrive
at each other for the first time
since campus and it's rocky
when he writes you to stay the
night (because what kind of
girl does he think) there is a
rage-letter I'm still yet to see
and silence sits between you
for weeks until he is at your
doorstep in your living room
refusing to sit down in your
mother's presence the skinny
moustached man who will
become my father lies prostrate
before grandma and offers to

take you flat-viewing that same
afternoon   says   something
ridiculous like *we could make
a home out of this* which only
you would love and from then
you are the pulse I know you to
be growing into yourself more
sudden than you can contain
each time into the flesh of a
new   feeling   like   a   seed
growing into a seed a promise
bursting a promise I want you
to know that this fullness is the
only   way   I   ever   wish   to
recognise you

EBI

III

VI

VII

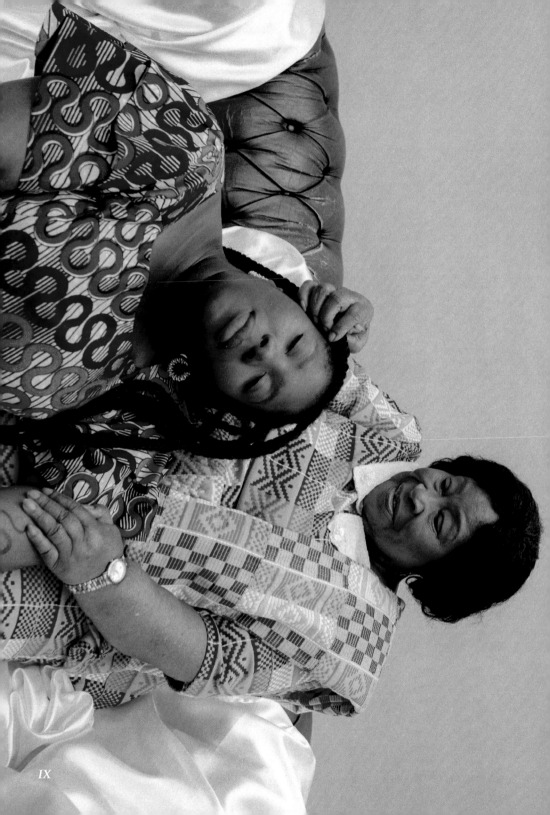

NICK MAKOHA

These two poems echo each other. They both speak of my exodus from Uganda. The first poem focuses on my mother and how she delivered me to safety. What my mother taught me in this act of bravery is how to fly. Flying is often defined as moving through the air using wings. As a writer with many allegiances, I am in a process of endless transformation, a person in perpetual flight. I often find myself pushing away from the grounded things that are familiar to me and taking leaps of faith. The second poem has a wider lens. It considers that my exodus from Uganda is a recurring story that could be replicated by others and that my personal story is an analogue for a broader experience.

When I was the Morning Bird

We awoke to spring, and I was thinking this:
what if I told you about my mother as if a river
was flowing by? Wings are not a metaphor
for exile but their print will surely leave a stain.
Once, as I fanned a firefly from my face, she taught
me about rising above the cascading mountains
of our country where nothing moves, where the
clouds slip away. In that picture I was myself,
as a tree is itself, as the sun is itself. Ask a woman
to dream and a river stands still. Here the world
becomes what it was before we knew it. Who can
bear to be some owned thing? This shadow of a bird,
this black woman with her mystic sweat, whose words
always knew how they wanted to begin, whose
thoughts were a map. That is why we are here
at the day's edge, having passed through rooms
of diminishing size – the village hall, a store cupboard
at the bus depot in Busia Town and the two back rooms
with no outside light at the airport terminal. They greet
us on our departure and as we arrive in the world over there.

A Reference

In those days I used the road as a spear
and the night as a cloak. We sang songs
to say our names, caught rainwater to wash
our clothes, walked the river's path to take us
home. Sometimes our teeth were knives
or a whistle and with the right person
a door to the tongue to bind ourselves
to the person who could fill us. For me
that was you, even when you took the
shape of the wind because you were
suspicious of what the day would hold
and its burden and its function and its
cypher and its entry and its reference.

Nick Makoha

BE MANZINI

There is something magical about the liminal space between truth and dreaming; I jigsawed pieces of stories of my paternal grand-parents from fragmented re-tellings, with an anxious prayer of creating something befitting them. I hope these poems are side by side in the way that my grandmother and grandfather came together to gift my recently departed Baba life. That my first foray into partly writing in Zulu is a deep bow to them and the hundreds that came before. It's a humbling thing to remember that generations of love and love-making that had to happen for us each to be here...that every human being is indeed a miracle. My prayer was that my musical thoughts did justice to the magic, miracles and love in my ancestors' lives.

Blessings

Sangoma / inyanga: shamans, healers, priests, and prophets that have been the backbone of Bantu communities.

My granddaddy
Fimbi
Sangoma crowned
Gesisa iKhago
one
who washes
the house
in milk
by the women
he healed
who wanted babies—
milk
from the cows
they gifted
in thanks
for enlivening
their homesteads.

Umzingeli / Oqoqayo: hunter-gatherer.

You could find a beast,
empty it of life
in a single arrow's flight.
Across your back,
shoulder to shoulder
with Elan;
matching skin,
blood-colour
cloth wrapped around
your waist,
your feet glittering

red
with Gweru soil.

Makhulambile (Zulu): 'let them speak'; ancestral home
to one branch of the Manzini family.

> I am searching
> for pieces of you
> as I walk.
> Feet pitted,
> pink from heat,
> moon showing its full belly.
> I am waiting for your face
> to burst the sky,
> a constellation
> that doesn't come.
> I'm calling the earth
> to unash you,
> the chime of the wind
> to carry your voice
> to harmonise
> the praise and prophecies.
> I am somehow
> here
> trying to fit
> all of you
> into a chorus
> *Umkhulu ubuso bakho*
> *esibhakabhakeni yenze line*
> *ukuze ngikwazi ukuphola...*

Khulu: grandparent or elder
Unkhulunkhulu: the divine or god

> I'm close.

> *Ngiyacela wena*
> heal me too.

Gogo[*]

i

There's an echo
that your clan
changed your name
to hide from the enemy.
But whiteness
took over the land
like rot on mourning fruit.

ii

Springstone and elegant,
beloved of Eland.
We danced in fields
to honour you.
Wore horns in carnival,
talked Talawa...
          praise songs
not always in words.

Tsike, basket weaver,
your fingers turned
blood-berry. Eyes
of midnight...   I dream
of you now
at the Limpopo
collecting willow
reeds, treading

---

*   Gogo is Zulu/Ndebeleß

Be Manzini

borders. Your birth
point between
three rivers...
           a glass triangle...
how did your voice sound?
Your gifting hands?
I can only look for you
in the mirror.

           iii

My father always spoke of you
in English; my heart listens
in Ndebele. I call you Grace
in both languages.

THEMBE MVULA

One of my concerns when writing these poems was the idea of how we wish to be remembered, and the extent of our ability to shape that. The tone of *Praise Poem for Makhulu*, a character portrait of my grandmother, nods to the tradition of Xhosa praise poetry. In my culture, bards, known as *imbongi*, are called on to convey the people's adoration of chiefs and their ancestors, among other things. This felt like a meaningful and exciting connection to make when writing a poem that honours an important matriarchal figure in mine and my family's lives.

Women's Work was my attempt to recapture one of the main displays of love I observed between my grandparents. Growing up, displays of affection through physical touch were uncommon. Instead, love coloured mundane moments like the one showcased in *Women's Work*. To write the former, I relied on information from my mother and old photographs to fill my knowledge and memory gaps. In the latter, I write from the perspective of my younger self, whose recollections of my late grandparents are more vivid and present.

Women's Work

grandma sits at the end of the bed where feet,
like a bunch of ripe bananas on a branch,
hang. his overgrown nails like mountain peaks
on toes like tiny worn out rocks that used to dance.
grandad feels love through her bony fingertips
pressing into his arches and bunions with zeal.
joy kindles in her eyes, radiates from her lips
a gentle fire, as she exfoliates his calloused heel
slowly, the way dawn disburdens night.
her devotion is in the perfect amount
of salt in beef and dumpling stew, crisp bite
of honey hued vetkoek. he cannot go without.
when she died, his memory began to decompose.
even then her love nursed him, head to toe.

Praise Poem for Makhulu

Though born near the small seaside town of Port Alfred,
you never ventured into the shallows, for fear of being

swallowed by the Indian ocean's arcane appetite for twins.
I knew you as *Makhulu*, but you lived up to a handful of other

names. Nombuyiselo from birth–
     to give back.
Nowethu from marriage–
     lady of our home, of our people.

Adorned in scarlet blazer, silver broach, black headscarf,
you and your army of mothers who never missed

Sunday service, cash inside your bra cup slipped
into collection or hands of a neighbour in need.

Neighbours would string outside the house to sip
your brew of umqombothi and brag about it after. Always

an extra plate of food on the side for any stranger
or friend who might grace our dinner time door.

You, domestic worker, sewer, seller of homemade smocks,
cinnamon skin, gold mines for eyes, could cause

a storm with your voice. Rescued me to find mine.
You, the responsible twin, matriarch of the Mvula's, gravity

of your kin. You raised your children's children, spoiled us,
slept beside us at night, taught us how to walk correctly.

Thembe Mvula

TANIA NWACHUKWU

Francis Onwuakpa, Christiana and Louis Nwachukwu, their physical bodies have been laid to rest but they are very much alive. Listening to, learning from and retelling their stories allows me to carve their spirits into the marrow of this realm. I feel like it is my job to find ways for them to be found, over and over again – through and beyond my own lifetime.

Oghe

We parked in my cousin's compound
  and in one of my aunties' houses,

my mother pointed: did you know
  that was your great-grandmother?

In the picture, my great-grandmother
  sits on a chair, surrounded by clay pots.

My mother once said we were descendants of
  potters. Withstanding high heat was coded

into our DNA. My mother used to take hot trays
  from the oven, bare hands, without flinching.

I held on to that for years, testing the weight
  of things passed down, things left behind,

the way Cousin Adaeze wears my grandmother's face,
  how my father's laugh echoes my grandfather's,

both calling back to someone before.
  Seeing my great-grandmother, framed simply

in the front room of extended family, I wanted to know
  if they knew that those pots weren't simple props.

That we are all clay, shaped by her hands.
  That nothing we have is ours alone.

Tania Nwachukwu

Things I Know to Be True

for you nne m, I miss you all the time x

I never heard a story about you
that didn't involve prayer.

Some say it was luck,
how men with greed for eyes
swarmed your compound,
flipped the tables in your home,
dragged you to the foot of the safe
and spared your life.

They knew nothing of daily bread.
How it lined your stomach
and filled you with conviction.
How your voice, unwavering
even in uncertainty
asked to forgive those
who trespassed against us.

The men with poison for mouths
tried every combination, every key.
Wore throats sore shouting at you,
at the lock. The safe refused.
Some say it was black magic.
How it stood defiant in the face of evil.
Onye Nkuzi, in name and practice.
Even rust became your disciple.

Some say it was God.
How the earth shook when you fell
to your knees. How you challenged him
to show his face. Reminded him

that you were his child,
that if he couldn't find you,
you were the one who looked like him—
face carved in his image,
folded over in fear and faith.

Your prayer formed somewhere
deep in your belly, heaven-bound
before reaching your mouth.
Some say it had spear-like precision,
splitting lock from safe
in one swift motion.

And those men,
how they ran.

---

*   *Onye Nkuzi* - 'person who teaches'/ teacher

                 Tania Nwachukwu

GBOYEGA ODUBANJO

With these poems, I wanted to focus on the way that places and languages merge within one's consciousness. The settings that I present take as much from London as they do from Lagos (or Ijebu-Ode or Ibadan), just as I imagine that, for my parents and those before them, they wished home could combine the structural assurances they sought in London with the warmth and community they left behind. But the act of trying to build a world for yourself, wherever that may be, is never easy. Always, the potential for joy is bound to the risk of danger. There are two specific moments that I tentatively hold together in my poem, *Function*, which attempt to speak to this thin line between joy and danger: the 1981 New Cross Fire which took the lives of 14 young black people during a house party; and the 1977 attack on Fela Kuti's Kalakuta Republic which would lead to the death of his mother.

Function

just a little room we had and it was our world
top notch residents we were   never did a madness
didn't once bowl in lathered and piss in the potpourri
no-one could ever say of us we didn't enjoy

especially when the barman came out from under the bed
and the mccoys were on the house   pennies in the jukebox
last entry was at two and then they locked us in

or did we lock ourselves in
declare independence as best you could with a tongue in your mouth
everyone clapping   the children picking money off the ground
putting it in black bags for the celebrants   elders putting up flags
because they said we couldn't paint the walls breaking clocks
when they said we had fifteen minutes left in the hall
we saw smoke   realised it was lit

was nang was heavy was bad was sick
the roof the roof on fire   water wasted on the drunk
blues and twos roused and wooing
a thousand soldiers at the door looking for their bit
of slap and tickle   mothers jumping out of windows
backs breaking in the dance   no doctors in the room

Gboyega Odubanjo

Compound

be sending the money and the land will be here waiting for you
first we will dig for the water then we will send for the goat and we will bless it
we will take care of everything or maybe you don't think we know what we are doing
the price the builder gave you is not a serious price unless you don't want joy
if you don't like the way the sun shines in the morning we can bring you a new one
the local guys will say you should pay tax but we can sort that one out
you want everything included school hospital transport we can build
there's nothing like government or policeman here everything we can do
if anyone should try to rob you believe me the smoke will clear before you hear pim
if you want the house to be a prayer a meal an ocean we can manage
there is space for you your children their children their concubines their ghosts
when you are coming let us know the diesel will be in the generator
the guinness will be cooking the family you don't know they will come and eat
only when they are full will they remember that the rain has finished

DAMILOLA OGUNRINDE

Spirituality embeds itself into all aspects of African life and culture. It determines how we interact with dreams, food, love, beauty and the future. These poems observe how our silence and spirituality have manifested in several generations of Nigerian elders. The stories of our grandparents traverse civil wars that they do not speak of and how external cultures have changed and remodelled which values we now hold dear.

South

Each year when we leave for Christmas
Mother rolls her eyes.
Father said our union is false,
yet there is no schism in our bed.
I do not know where I end, and you begin.
I once ate an unblessed Kola.
Your father will not meet my eye.
It is not about the Kola, you said:
it is about Western silence.

Each year we go to the south by road.
Father hides his head in the paper;
Mother says rituals are diabolical,
tilting her head tie as she leaves for a wedding.
Your mother smiles and nods her head,
accommodates me without engaging.
Your grandfather's house stands tall by the river,
black rain causes villagers to live in dread.
You join your uncles as they pass Kola in prayers,
I retreat to a silent place to rest.

Last year we didn't go to Atlanta for summer;
you said you are building your first house.
My father recommended a place by the laguna,
but your father has gifted you a plot in the south.
I do not comprehend, yet understand,
that our son will build his haven.
The soil of his fathers, a land that remembers.
They said it was hundreds; we thought it was thousands;
the avoidance in your father's eyes says it was millions.
This year we will south again for Christmas.

Echoes of Beauty

I

Elders did not gather
and cowries were not counted,
yet Olodumare announced her
Arinola, born to wealth.
Before beauty was defined
by imperial metrics, the spirits
echoed her name: oriki
like no other, pillar that upholds,
arms that embrace, songs
to celebrate her frame.
When asked for their star
the whole town pointed
to her. Arinola,
kissed by God himself.

II

Daughter of the soil,
no mere balm for skin,
ori was her healer.
Soon spirits stopped singing.
The land had been plundered.
Olodumare retreated to His throne.
Arinola kept dancing
to the music inside her.
How do you move with grace
when in pain? Arinola smiles,

nodding as she whispers:
Battles are won before they begin.
Rehearse victory in faith and dreams;
beauty's source lies within.

III

Now we, her daughters, seek beauty
in the faces of those who plunder us.
Rubbing ori with no ritual,
filtered frames concealing scars.
We move our hips to songs with no spirit,
we do not have our mothers' tongue,
we feast on algorithms that doom us;
rule us out, crushing strong bones.
Yet, in the midst of imperial chaos
our search proves Olodumare's ear
waking to Arinola's prayers
crafting new songs within us.
Beauty is not from contoured spaces.
Looted lands can be restored.
Ayanfe, rub ori slowly.
Affirm yourself as you do.

HIBAQ OSMAN

When I received the brief, I wondered how best to write about ancestry and lineage in a way that didn't push me further from history, or romanticise a life I didn't live. The poems I selected are based on stories told to me about my grandparents, the Somali seafaring tradition and illness in our communities. I share these poems in the spirit of defending what we love and using that energy to carry us all forward into new experiences. *Before Them, We* honours our elders and in these poems I hope to have created further links between us all.

Isn't That How It Goes? When Everything You Love Is Bound to Leave, Don't You Reach for the Door First?

1. On her dresser, the faint scent of perfume. Promises of men she'd given up. Stocky, strange and regretful men send letters through her windowsill. 'If not together, how?' they write.

   If not now, never she tells herself.

2. She toys with the idea of another life. Growing full-bellied into The Mother, the Forever, the Endlessness she is yet to know. Won't it all be worth it in the end?

3. Grandma is known for not keeping to the city. Stone and tarmac are no way to live. In younger years, she was wanted in the way only written of in folktales. Young suitors from afar with thick skin. She'd tell her sisters *he's come to see you*, skipping through the gate. While neighbours watched and talked.

4. We still are not sure how they met. They rewrote the story, endlessly. Perhaps it was a mocking-bird that led them together. She would argue it was a double-headed snake. On good days he would say love overtook him. On bad, he'd say a falling branch must have blessed him with a madness. This is how all their stories go.

5. Before the adhaan and the goats woke, a bottle of perfume was placed under the shade of her tin roof. Bird call stopped. The air held still. The long morning was woven into the sky.

6. She does not wear rouge, kohl or earrings. With gifted scent and a sense of change she makes a choice. *This is all I will need. This will be enough. Heavens and earth in one bottle. I will have it blessed. I will wear it to sleep. I will accept.*

7. And so they began. And so we were destined to live.

Keeping a Lighthouse

I have been waiting at the shore
the way a woman waits for grand return:
the casket drop, the breath
that only exists on Sundays.

When the mist settles around your frame
and I am certain it is you,
I will scatter all doubts of God.
I will tell the longing it cannot stay,
that it will not make a nest in my hollow home

I have been searching, long hours,
the way fishermen do,
arms wide enough to net
the vastness between sand and waves.
Every goodbye has been its own shipwreck.
In the rubble, we were shining trinkets.

When you return to dock I wonder
what it took to disappear into yourself.
At night, I envy the demons that perch
upon your shoulders, most attentive of lookouts,
those that will not be swatted away,
the fact that they endure both in your head
and in your hand —

how they can follow you out to sea
and exist in all the forms I can't.

Hibaq Osman

Nii Ayikwei Parkes

In my family, you often find the old men holding court, telling stories. The thing I noticed as a child is that they were mostly telling stories about the women in the family, they were hype men before hype men were Hip Hop. I continue in that tradition here. The story of African men is often told in images of their brutalised bodies, and everyone offers opinions on what captions they should carry: What is true? What is prejudice? What is strength? What is frailty? What is human, what animal? Rarely in the captions is an account of the labour of running alongside and catching the shrapnel from the constant fire the Black male body is subjected to. What does it take to be the child of, the companion of, the nurturer of, the restorer of a being marked for target practice? Maybe this is why I was always destined to carry on tradition, to speak of Grace and the fabric of fortitude handed down from generation to generation.

Grace

It is outstretched, exposed
trunks that remind me I am away
from home, their dark arms holding

up morning sky, betraying a history
of fallen leaves – yellow and brown
supplicants that answer to autumn's call

and fall with grace, twirling in eddies
to settle with a whisper of a curtsey.
Hours slip into memory, conjure other leaves,

larger leaves, the rubber plant's shiny
ovals that we split, bent and sutured
into nurse's caps to place on our tight curls

and pretend to be Grandma: she of silvered hair;
she of the resonant laugh that carried and carried;
she who had dozens of babies named after her;

she who nursed an Englishman back to health,
who would later take care of her son in London
without having to brave the strange seasons

herself; she whose son spared her the truth
of how the BMW Mr Pertwee sold him for next
to nothing led to him being accosted more times

Nii Ayikwei Parkes

than he could remember; she whose graceful smile
spread like sunlight when he told her the loud rumble
of the car is what made his new fiancée notice him.

And what is grace if not the coaxing of
beauty from the stiff uniforms a land throws
at you, if not new dreams from fallen leaves?

The Soviet Coat

I already knew you didn't sleep
some nights, but that's a fraction
of the story, of the horde of sighs
migration placed beneath your tongue
and sealed with a nurse's smile.

It is at parties thrown in our names, where
we were sent to bed early as grown ups
unpacked their full selves to bend
to syncopations of songs from home, that
we overheard the first notes of your range:

how you turned up to work, sharp and pleated
at six a.m. without having slept a sliver
after nights criss-crossing London
to shake your Fattie at parties, Carl Malcolm
playing in both African and Caribbean houses.

I already knew you didn't sleep some nights,
but it is only in the wake of heartbreaks,
when I'm cutting onions one afternoon,
that we chew over the burden of sun
streaming through a window that you own;

what it means for a country to welcome you
and then forbid you from having children
in the home you rent, forcing new mothers
to farm their children out to the country
to walk lanes that will rattle with stones

Nii Ayikwei Parkes

as they rise into the fullness of their shadows.
Nothing is accidental. Buying a house
was necessary even if it distilled a dentist's dream
into a nurse's hand. Even if the local school
wasn't ready for boys bright with Vaseline®.

I already knew you didn't sleep through
some nights, but I wonder now who could,
knowing what you know, having seen
friends collect their babies from sitters,
filthy from the day's excretions, faces

marked by dried tears because the carers
would not countenance comforting babies
so dark, so alien, so strong in voice –
instead, they left them swaddled in corridors,
closed doors to drown them out.

Acts so cold that you, raised in boarding schools
because of your mother's travels, should find them
difficult to stomach, and even the thick Soviet coat
she gifted you from her Eastern itineraries
could not keep out the shivers as you told me.

Yomi Sode

Before Them, We, provided an opportunity I had subconsciously put in the back of my mind for a while. These pieces in particular speak to the complexities of my grandmother. A woman, an elder that I love very much and if I'm honest, someone I don't know much about, due to me leaving Nigeria at a young age. The distance from her and the other pieces of me left behind in Nigeria has been impactful.

I question the space I write from a lot and in this case, I'm thankful for this experience in opening the room for exploration. I noticed my moral codes, my Western lens, my silence and culturally, how these matters played into each other.

I return to these pieces and I find new ways to unpack them. I wonder where love lies within them and most importantly, I search for the meaning.

Deborah

The afternoon Grandma punched her house help
in the chest, the girl's left foot shifted back,

digging into the floor for balance. The girl's shoulder
blades caved towards each other as if to sprout wings.

Her lips chiselled forward, then stiffened.
She bit her tongue before holding breath,

praying Grandma would look elsewhere so she could rub
the burn and cry a cry quick enough to go unnoticed.

Grandma stared, waiting for another reason. But the girl
stood still. Her anger, churning inside like Aunty's Pot of Ogi.

Pepe

You must have plenty Pepe, Grandma says, throwing hands in the air as she continues, *They argued yesterday, by the gate.* It's rain season in Nigeria and I've been lucky to have had so much sun in the past week. Electricity out for the past two days, food has gone off and the bottled water has warmed. What's none of our business has found its way into our front room. *Why do you think she walked off alone, did they not come in here together? He told her to go home, with her Pepe-less self! Like that!*

In my eyes, the Kunle family can do no wrong. Femi and Florence, Team Double F, The Fast and The Furious, Jay Z & Beyonccce, Clark & Lois. Lauded as the 'Barak Obama' of the village, Professor Femi Kunle is held in high regard amongst the poor and rich of Ibadan and surrounding areas alike. Houses in America and London, a hotel chain in Nigeria and rumours he would (one day) run for Senator. A community man who built a tap outside his house so the less fortunate could collect clean water for free. On sunny days, kids with buckets fight for water, parents and passers-by giving thanks.

Florence Kunle (just like Michelle) is calm, but fierce. An activist fighting for women's rights to equal pay and health care in Nigeria while supporting Femi's battle against corruption in government houses. Florence owns a nursery in the heart of the village to support struggling mothers. Yet Florence lacks what Grandma calls 'Pepe'— her Afro-lingua franca for sexy, pretty and confident.

Pepe goes with anything, and any talk, if you know how it works:
Pepe doesn't run for the bus, the bus runs for Pepe.
Pepe doesn't RSVP, the tables are just cleared.
Pepe does not queue! Kai, the queue is jumped upon Pepe's arrival.

Yomi Sode

Grandma embodies this with ease— passionate advocate for God, looking good and being acknowledged for looking good. *Junior! You see your Grandfather eh, the only thing he did not want was Pepe on my lips and fingernails, ah! Baba hated it! Ah he did not like. He wanted natural, a natural woman eh, that was my Pepe. Junior! Imagine, Uncle told his wife to watch how your Grandma dresses. Especially how I wrap my gele on my head.*

I want my western mouth to run before I catch it. To defend Florence Kunle, Michelle Obama of the village. Campaigner, activist and entrepreneur. The shoulders on which Femi stands. Mother. Wife. To question Grandma's warped reality of success. Surely, all of this is the definition of Pepe. A woman, confident enough to challenge the status quo, a leader. Is that not 'Pepe' enough? Grandma stares at me, and for a moment I imagine saying all of these things to her. Instead, I say nothing. As if my voice has yet to break.

You must have plenty Pepe o, look good for your husband and cook for your husband, or else he will leave you for someone else, someone that does not focus their life, on other things.

There's a math at play here. Though my age is acknowledged, it doesn't equal respect deserved. Though Florence is thriving in her independence, it doesn't mean her husband won't be seen as weak for not having his wife in control. Grandma evaluates the division of loyalties, the subtraction of a wife and the addition of someone new. She wants Florence to remain a wife— to be something else risks too much. In spite of all her gossip and brag, Grandma is checking for Florence.

Junior, listen. On my 80th birthday celebration. I walked into church with my new Ankara. There was a woman - Ife Labake that was celebrating her 80th the following month. My son, do you know that the pastor personally went to Ife and asked if she could wear a similar Ankara to the one I wore on my 80th!

Ah! PEPE! Grandma shouts
PLENTY PEPE O, Mummy joins.

We laugh.

I think of Florence. I think of Grandma, and wonder how she felt the day she locked her ambitions away in favour of love. A different kind of security.

Yomi Sode

MICHELLE TIWO

I'd asked my mum about her grandad once and she had very little information. That pushed me on to interview my Uncle Kofi, mum's older brother, who revealed a history of displacement, resilience and restarts. The poem, *This, is all I have* is a verbatim piece transcribed from part of that hour-long conversation. When *Gnamato set roots down in Klouvindonou* is a combination of the little my mum knew about her grandfather and a simplified version of the story my uncle recounted. With both poems, I wanted to work with space to emphasise and highlight what happens to rich (hi)stories, such as my ancestors', when little is shared by and amongst their descendants and imagination has to fill in the blanks. Excited to finally know something about my maternal lineage, these poems are an opportunity to allow their beginnings, at the least, to be told and known.

This, Is All I Have

according to my uncles, she was from the
North of Togo, very far. there was a war she
lived. after the war
the winners got to take
our great-great-grandmother and, some other
young girls, as a gift
On their way walking she got lost
not knowing where she's coming from, not knowing where she's going.
just wandering
sleeping living like a proper animal. she was spotted
by my great-great-grandfather. He nursed her
then married her. Nobody knew

nothing about t I her the only thing we knew
her name, Nana.

Michelle Tiwo

When Gnamato Set Roots Down in Klouvindońou

When Gnamato set roots
down in Klouvindońou

Mum said: He sent for all his sisters
                                       to prove to his new neighbours

He was the most beautiful man.   he came from somewhere

He was successful too, I think...   as testament that leaving his family at [13?]
                                      was worth the [years? miles?] given up on the
                                      journey.

He had his own land and farm   Finally, a home to bury the laden mocking of
                                      not knowing, or having, a history to speak of.

in this old village,   Here, he could see what it meant to live and
                                      build undaunted.

somewhere in Togo.   At last, the relentless ghosts
                                      of his wicked old neighbours' folklores
                                      claiming him son of an alien
                                      bush woman's beast baby;
                                      [weeks? months?] after his father died;
                                      could stop and be laid to rest.

Hodan Yusuf

I was approached for this anthology just a few months after my father's passing and it felt like a sign. It gave me an opportunity to begin to confront my tremendous grief and give tribute in poetry form, not just to my *Aabo* but to all of my forebears. Our elders and ancestors are not only key to our existence in a biological sense, but also provide us with a sense of placement in the world. So I wanted to show how even when they were not aware of their future legacies, they were leaving us trails in their paths. I feel there is an amalgamation of our timeline and their timeline in a way that is often hard to express. I did my best to capture that interconnectedness which still feels tangible even after their passing.

No We Before You

Without you, there is no me;
Without you
Having been before me.

None would have been able to
Become
After you.
Without you
There's no me.

And without you
There's no We
On which to lean
And to belong.

And without you
It would be a long road
Leading
To no home.

And because of you,
We get to be.

Before us
You were
Untethered, young,

Free and travelling
All lands,

But with every compass you used
We were guided home.

Unbeknownst to you,
One day you'd be

Them
Who came
Before
We.

Indelible

We move but we leave
An indelible mark.
We have been changed
Or forced to
And have changed
Them too.

Changed
This place
And all the places we have been.
Landed on,
Landed in.

These shores
Holding more than our skins,
Holding stories and humans within
Wombs and loins
Which bore people
Who will witness
Long, long ago
But also tomorrow.

Everywhere they went,
We were with them.
Every slur and hurt
We felt and heard
And still we feel
Every laugh
Passed down
Through this bloodline.

Sometimes we trespass our own histories
Into chapters we were not meant to read.
They would not want us to feel it all
But all of it is etched upon us.

When the little white child said "Mummy, it speaks!"
We were witness.
And when Johnny and his men commandeered the house
We were witness.
And when they fenced off neighbours from each other
Placing some in cages
We were witness.

When she held the cries of her labour pains in
From a "shame" that should have never been,
Biting on her clothes instead,
We were witness.

We move,
They move.
And places can never be the same
After we have been,
And they have been
Marked
Outside
And within.

And they witness

When we make homes
From places that demand our blood
But not our laughter;
Pain and never joy.
They bear witness
When joy is found

Hodan Yusuf

And pain is healed
And laughter shared.
And they witness
That their own will one day
Recreate
Their own indelible marks.

BELINDA ZHAWI

The poems *Msasa: Matriarch of the Woodland* & *Matrilineal Lines* reflect on the distance and silence between the poet and their mothers. Both poems are a recollection of & meditation on ancestry and home.

Msasa… is a lament for the possibilities that were never realised whilst also celebrating the beauty of what once was shared between the poet & the deceased. In a quieter way it is also a reflection on borders, movement and their effects on how we communicate with our 'home' lands.

Matrilineal Lines takes its inspiration from the *Book of the Generations of Adam* in Genesis 5 of the Bible and Shona praise poetry where patrilineal lines are used to trace ancestry. In both texts the father's name is held with more importance and the mothers seem to be phantoms.

Msasa: Matriarch of the Woodland

i

    I imagine you on a makeshift bed
under the thin, red-leaved, msasa tree
    opposite the kitchen,
waiting for the medicine to kick in, chase the aches
    that settle in your bones.
    I imagine you dozing into,
    a dream of Sekuru's watery eyes
& tar lips blackened by decades
    of newspaper-rolled tobacco.
    Telling him you will see him soon.

ii

    I remember you, the rainy season
    of '98, lying on a rupasa
    under the flowering msasa tree,
    leaves greened by rains,
    chewing stick in one corner of your mouth.

    I remember you full of crooked smiles;
    dressed languid, feet dusty
    from a day spent hoeing fields,
    remember asking you
    why my parents no longer looked
    each other in the eye.

    You replied
    your eyes are too fast, child,
    your eyes are too fast.

I remember you,
dry season of '99, your arms
two warm rivers that seeped into the cracks
of February divorces,
    unfinished conversations & unvoiced gripes.

    I remember you being the strength that kept me.
    Now - there you go
    strolling down to where you started,

    returning to where you can finally see
    yourself

iii

My papers arrived from the Home Office
to say I was no longer alien
in this foreign land that knows neither
rainy nor dry season - just rain for its sake.
Flooded with relief
I imagined finally coming to you,
to sit under the young msasa, watch chickens,
drink pots of loose leaf brews,
watch you knit, listen to you curse
my mother's cooking, smile & ignore you.

Instead, I am alone, five thousand miles away,
on my bedroom floor, black & white
photos from your youth on my chest.
Outside, through the window,
my mother's listless pink rosebush
leans against our tired fence.
Moments before sleep, I trace your face
beneath my eyelids;
picture you
stiff, in a morgue.

Belinda Zhawi

iv

These days I fail to remember your face.
It's winter soon.   It will be colder soon.
        My fingers will numb & stiffen
soon, making it hard to cup
the warmth of a hot drink.
A tension in the shoulders.   Stiff
     in the joints   counting
          down
   seconds   to   the   white
   of their bones.

I will be cold one day soon,
    like you.

Matrilineal Lines

"De nigger woman is de mule uh de world so fur as Ah can see..."
Janie Crawford, Their Eyes Were Watching God

Ini ndini Ratidzo,
first daughter *wa* Konesai, born third
on the third day *wa* Mandipei – the one
who *knows* how to alloy voice & tongue
into a burning scythe that cuts through
all levels of self-esteem. *wa* Munodei also
known as *moyo dombo,* stone heart, who
married twice when women masqueraded
as birthing chambers in the dry seasons &
in the rainy seasons as ploughmen, babies
on back - nestled inside bold print cotton
wrappers. Daughter of Hatifi-kuno whose mind
was the riven portico of a broken home, who lived
what it is to be *mule of the world.* Rock,
born stuck in the ground to bear
the sun's blaze & the drench of rainy days.
Day in, day out, day in, day out.
Day in, day out, day in, day out -
the sun's blaze & the drench of rainy days.
Born stuck in the ground to bear
what it is to be *a mule of the world.* Rock,
was the riven portico of a broken home, who lived in
wrappers. Daughter of Hatifi-kuno, whose mind
on (sat on her) back. Nestled inside bold print cotton
in the rainy seasons. As ploughmen. Babies.
As birthing chambers in the dry seasons &
married twice when women masqueraded.
Known as *moyo dombo,* stone heart, who was
all levels of self-esteem. *wa* Munodei, also
a burning scythe that cuts through,

Belinda Zhawi

who *knows* how to alloy voice & tongue.
(Born) on the third day, *wa* Mandipei – the one,
first daughter *wa* Konesai. Born third –
ini ndini Ratidzo.

EBI

Image X: long may delight consume
Image XI: iya wa, iya wa, iya wa

BIOGRAPHIES

Tolu Agbelusi

Tolu Agbelusi is the author of Locating Strongwoman (Jacaranda, 2020). A Nigerian British poet, playwright, educator and lawyer, she was nominated for the 2021 Forward Prize for Best Single Poem, & shortlisted for the 2018 White Review Poetry Prize. Her work has been published widely including in Wildness Journal, Aké Review, White Review, Pittsburgh Poetry Review, Brittle Paper and Peepal Tree's Filligree Anthology. She has also performed on stages including Cheltenham Lit Festival, Stanza International Poetry Festival Lagos International Poetry Festival Poetry Africa & Women of the World Festival.

Gabriel Akamo

Gabriel is a Nigerian-British poet, actor, facilitator, and creative producer based in London. As a multi-disciplinary practitioner, Gabriel's work often leads him beyond poetry and performance, often drawing on his background in both theatre and academic Philosophy, and his writing currently explores faith, relationships, and his overlapping identities.

Siana Bangura

Siana Bangura is a writer, producer, performer and community organiser hailing from South East London, now living, working, and creating between London and the West Midlands. Siana is the founder and former editor of Black British Feminist platform, No Fly on the WALL; she is the author of poetry collection, 'Elephant'; and the producer of '1500 & Counting', a documentary film investigating deaths in custody and police brutality in the UK and the founder of Courageous Films. Siana works and campaigns on issues of race, class, and gender and their intersections and is currently working on projects focusing on climate change, the arms trade, and state violence. Her recent works include the short film 'Denim' and the play, 'Layila!'. She was an artist-in-residence at the Birmingham Rep Theatre throughout 2019, a Jerwood supported artist throughout 2020, and is the co-host of 'Behind the Curtains' podcast, produced in partnership with English Touring Theatre (ETT) and host of 'People Not War' podcast, produced in partnership with Campaign Against Arms Trade (CAAT). Across her vast portfolio of work, Siana's mission is to help move marginalised voices from the margins, to the centre.

Dzifa Benson

Dzifa Benson is a multi-disciplinary artist whose work intersects science, art, the body and ritual which she explores through poetry, prose, theatre-making, performance, essays, and criticism. She has performed her work nationally and internationally in many contexts such as: artist in residence at the Courtauld Institute of Art; producer of a poetry in performance event responding to David Hockney's work in Tate Britain; producer and host of a literature and music experience in the Dissenters Gallery of Kensal Green Cemetery and core artist in BBC Africa Beyond's cross-arts project, Translations. Her work has been published and presented in The Poetry Review, the Guardian, the Financial Times, the Telegraph, the Royal Opera House, the Bush Theatre and the House of Commons. She is a widely published poet whose most recent publication is in Staying Human, the latest in Bloodaxe Books' celebrated series of anthologies. Dzifa abridged the National Youth Theatre's 2021 production of Othello in collaboration with Olivier award-winning director Miranda Cromwell and is working on a commissioned play, Black Mozart/White Chevalier. She was creative producer on the schools' programme of Estuary 2021 Festival and curated a poetry sound installation for the main programme of the festival. Dzifa has an MA in Text & Performance from Birkbeck and RADA and is also a Ledbury Poetry Critic.

Clementine Burnley

Clementine E Burnley is a feminist migrant mother, writer and community organiser. She lives in Edinburgh. Her work has appeared or is upcoming in Magma, the National Flash Fiction Anthology and The Centifictionist. She's a 2021 Sky Arts Award Winner, an alumnus of Obsidian Foundation and a 2021 Edwin Morgan Second Life Grantee.

Ola Elhassan

Ola Elhassan is a Sudanese poet and electrical engineer. Sometimes her poetry experiments with and about music. You can read her work in journals like Sawti, Inkwell, and PANK magazine or watch her performances online from open mics and jazz nights in London where she's based.

Inua Ellams

Born in Nigeria, Inua Ellams is a poet, playwright & performer, graphic artist & designer and founder of: The Midnight Run (an arts-filled, night-time, urban walking experience.), The Rhythm and Poetry Party (The R.A.P Party) which celebrates poetry & hip hop, and Poetry + Film / Hack (P+F/H) which celebrates Poetry and Film. Identity, Displacement & Destiny are reoccurring themes in his work, where he tries to mix the old with the new: traditional African oral storytelling with contemporary poetics, paint with pixel, texture with vector. His books are published by Flipped Eye, Akashic, Nine Arches, Penned In The Margins, Oberon & Methuen.

Ibrahim Hirsi

Ibrahim Hirsi is a student, writer and peer researcher for the Centre for Mental Health. A digital Somali cultural archivist and independent researcher, his writings explore changes in Somali culture from colonialism till now. His work has appeared in PBLJ and he has worked as a consultant on Asmaa Jama's interactive short film "Before We Disappear".

Asmaa Jama

Asmaa Jama is a danish born Somali artist, poet and co-founder of Dhaqan Collective, a feminist art collective. They have been published in print and online in places like Ambit, ANMLY and The Good Journal. Asmaa's work has been translated into French, Swahili, Somali, Spanish and Portuguese. Most recently they were shortlisted for the Brunel African Poetry Prize and longlisted for the National Poetry Competition. Asmaa is an inaugural alumni of Obsidian Foundation. And is a Cave Canem 'Star Shine and Clay' Fellow.

Janet Kofi-Tsekpo

Janet Kofi-Tsekpo's work has been widely published in anthologies and magazines, including New Poetries V (Carcanet), Ten: New Poets (Bloodaxe), The Best British Poetry 2012 (Salt), Red (Peepal Tree), Bittersweet: Contemporary Black Women's Poetry (Women's Press), Poetry Review, PN Review, Wasafiri, Magma and elsewhere. Her chapbook Yellow Iris (University of Nebraska/Akashic Books) was part of the Eight New-Generation African Poets series edited by Kwame Dawes & Chris Abani and launched at the PEN World Voices Festival in New York.

Esther Kondo

Esther Kondo is a poet, writer, and experimental poetry filmmaker. They are a Barbican Young Poet 18/19, Black Obisidian fellow, Ledbury Critic, and incoming Cornell University MFA in poetry student. They have performed their poetry amongst other places at the Roundhouse, Literary Colloquium Berlin, and the Barbican.

Sarah Lasoye

Sarah is a poet and writer from London. She is an alumna of the Barbican Young Poets and a current member of Octavia – Poetry Collective for Women of Colour. Her debut chapbook, Fovea / Ages Ago, was published by Hajar Press in April 2021.

Nick Makoha

Nick Makoha is the founder of the Obsidian Foundation and winner of the 2021 Ivan Juritz Prize and 2021 Poetry London Prize. His 2017 debut collection, Kingdom of Gravity, was shortlisted for the Felix Dennis Prize for Best First Collection and was one of the Guardian's best books of the year. Nick is a Cave Canem Graduate Fellow and the Complete Works alumnus. He won the 2015 Brunel International African Poetry Prize and the 2016 Toi Derricotte & Cornelius Eady Prize for his pamphlet Resurrection Man. His poems have appeared in the Cambridge Review, New York Times, Poetry Review, The Rialto, Poetry London, TriQuarterly Review, Boston Review, Callaloo, and Wasafiri. He is a trustee for the Arvon Foundation and the Ministry of Stories, and a member of Malika's Poetry Kitchen collective.

Be Manzini

Be is known for her ability to create universal and nurtuting spaces as a workshop facilitator. A writer and speaker who has been resident at the Southbank Centre, a regular oanelist for film, judge for the innovative Visionary Honors Awards, Manzini is also the Director of Caramel Feilm Club, spolighting Black talent and supporting diversity. Her published work appears in various anthologies including 'Red' edited by Kwame Dawes. She has been commisisned to write for theatre Royal, Hoxton Hall, Autograph B, Tamasha as well as performing for leading poetry organisations such as Apples & Snakes. Manzini's poetry films have shown at the Royal Festival Hall, ICA, BFI and various cinemas and film festivals in the UK and abroad.

Thembe Mvula

Thembe Mvula is a South African writer and poet; an alum of the Roundhouse Poetry Collective, Barbican Young Poets and the inaugural Obsidian Foundation retreat. Her work often explores relationships, intergenerational trauma, healing, and home. She self-published her debut pamphlet, We that Wither Beneath, in 2019 and is currently undertaking a masters in Creative Writing at the University of Oxford.

Tania Nwachukwu

Tania Nwachukwu is an Igbo Actor, Performer, Writer and Educator, born and raised in London. She is the co-founder of Black in the Day, a Barbican Young Poets alum, a member of Octavia Poetry Collective and an MA Tutor at Mountview Academy of Theatre Arts and Royal Central School of Speech & Drama.

Gboyega Odubanjo

Gboyega Odubanjo is a British-Nigerian poet born and raised in East London. He is a Roundhouse Resident Artist and his debut pamphlet, While I Yet Live, was published by Bad Betty Press in 2019.

Damilola Ogunrinde

Damilola Ogunrinde is a poet born in Lagos. She explores the infusion of culture into adopted spirituality and its impact on the mind-body connection. Her writing has been influenced by Yoruba folklore and the customs of oral tradition.

Hibaq Osman

Hibaq Osman is a Somali writer born and based in London. Her first pamphlet 'A Silence You Can Carry' was published under Out-Spoken Press in 2015. In 2020, Hibaq released her first full poetry collection 'where the memory was' with Jacaranda Books.

Nii Ayikwei Parkes

Nii Ayikwei Parkes, is a Ghanaian-British producer and writer. A 2007 recipient of Ghana's ACRAG award for poetry, he has won acclaim as a children's author, poet, broadcaster and novelist - most notably the Prix Laure Bataillon for the French translation of his novel Tail of the Blue Bird, (Cape, 2009). Twice featured on London's Poems on the Underground, Nii Ayikwei's ballast series from his début poetry collection The Makings of You (Peepal Tree, 2010) was described by Ali Smith as "an astonishing, powerful remix of history and language and the possibilities of both". His latest book of poetry, The Geez is a Poetry Book Society Recommendation, was longlisted for the Rathbones Folio Prize, and shortlisted for the Walcott Prize.

Yomi Sode

Yomi is a Nigerian British writer, performer, and facilitator. He is a recipient of the Jerwood Compton Poetry fellowship 2019 and has read his poems internationally at various festivals, as well as performed his debut solo show (COAT) to sold-out audiences. Yomi has been published in Rialto Magazine, The Poetry Review, Bare lit and 10: Poets of the New Generation, as well as a contribution in SAFE: On Black British Men reclaiming space. Yomi is a member of Malika's Poetry Kitchen and a Complete Works Alumni. His Debut poetry collection, MANORISM will be published in spring 2022 by Penguin Press.

Michelle Tiwo

Michelle Tiwo is a queer non-binary Nigerian/Togolese writer and performer. Their work explores familial dynamics, identity, religion and what it means to be a first-generation Afrobrit raised in Sarf East London. With work spanning across radio, poetry, theatre, film and music, including Poetry Film Hack with Inua Ellams and Sistren podcast- there's no art form off-limits when it comes to fully realising the perspective of this emo with a sunshine aura.

Hodan Yusuf

Hodan Yusuf is a poet, writer, playwright and actress. She is a multimedia freelance journalist and a mediator and trainer in conflict resolution. Hodan has a BA Hons in Human Geography & Environmental Policy and a Diploma in Journalism. She has a MSc in Conflict Resolution & Mediation Studies from the University of London. Hodan has delivered workshops, spoken at and read her poetry at many universities, events and festivals. This includes IHRC, York University, Oxford University, University of East London, Muslim Institute, BareLit Festival, UK Parliament, British Library, University of Exeter, Amnesty International, the Tate Gallery and others. In 2019, Hodan's screen debut acting role saw her land a part in a J.J. Abrams & Warner Bros production. Hodan wrote, directed and performed her first play in 2020, for an International theatre festival screened live on Zoom from London, Delhi and San Francisco. Her essay "Waiting to Exhale - The Scarcity of Safe Spaces" was published this year 2021, in the anthology Cut From the Same Cloth. Hodan continues to develop her craft as an actor while working on her debut poetry collection.

Belinda Zhawi

Belinda Zhawi is a Zimbabwean literary & sound artist. She is the author of Small Inheritances (ignitionpress, 2018) & South of South East (Bad Betty Press, 2019), co-founder of literary arts platform BORN:FREE & experiments with sound/text performance as MA.MOYO. Her work has been broadcast & published on various platforms including The White Review, NTS Live, Boiler Room & BBC Radio 3, 4 & 6. Belinda hosts Juju Fission (RTM FM), a monthly radio broadcast. She lives & works in South East London.